The Floorshow:
origins of a theatrical art

DOUGLAS WILLIAM WOODS

© 2016
DOUGLAS WILLIAM WOODS
ALL RIGHTS RESERVED

DEDICATION

For My Dad and Mom,

Roy and Erna Woods,

and Lyn, Pam, and Roy

CONTENTS

	Acknowledgments	i
1	INTRODUCTION	Page 1
	EARLY HISTORY OF MASQUES	
2	AN OVERVIEW OF THE STRUCTURE OF FLOORSHOWS	Page 24
3	THE LAS VEGAS PRODUCTION OF A FLOORSHOW	Page 44
4	THE FUTURE OF THE FLOORSHOWS	Page 93
5	Bibliography	Page 99

Cover Design by Masa Homma

ACKNOWLEDGMENTS

The University of Akron, School of Dance, Theatre, and Arts Administration:

James Slowiak, Durand Pope, Adel Migid, and Lisa Lazar

David Morgenstern, Shirley Morgenstern-Topilow, and Carl Topilow

Lido Colleague, Miranda Coe

Family and Friends,

Regine Mallath,

Masa and Pam Homma,

Archie and Diana Smith,

Jason Reddock

Career Transitions For Dancers; Joanne Devito, Linda Bunch, and Ann Barry

Ginny Poehling, and Lisa M. Jacob at the Las Vegas News Bureau.

Las Vegas Convention and Visitor's Authority

Frederic Apcar Productions

David Strow, and Lynn Jax, Boyd Gaming Corporation

Gary Thompson, Caesar's Entertainment

CHAPTER I

INTRODUCTION

The floorshow, commonly referred to as a musical revue, is a theatrical production with a large ensemble of lavishly costumed dancers and singers. From the late 1880s on, the Parisian cabaret influenced the evolution of the American musical revue, Hollywood movies, and other entertainment forms. On July 2, 1958, the Lido de Paris's *C'est Magnifique* established the floorshow as a theatrical art in Las Vegas. This thesis will explore the origins and history of the floorshow and its influence on other performing arts.

Early History of Masques

The floorshow is a theatrical art that depicts the cultural history of the past, where masques provided an interaction between the classes. Records from the later Renaissance period (1458–1550) indicate that the Italian court presented court theatre pieces known as *intermezzi* during lavish masques. These *intermezzi* introduced the processional-step for nobility and guests, and later to professional dancers in a show of steps and athletic routines. Though the *intermezzi* were an inter-act at the masques, they were usually dramatic pieces with music and dance that often lasted as long as the main acts. Several Italian dance masters of the period kept track of the practice hours required for learning the combinations of steps and for developing natural abilities. Guglielmo Ebreo da Pesaro was a dance master, choreographer, and author of *De practica seu arte tripudii* (On the Practice or Art of Dancing), published in 1463. Pesaro listed the important principles of dance and described five elements as the qualities necessary for dancers: posture, musicality, style, memory, and the ability to count. As he described it, the *pavana* (processional) step began on a whole count; there was also a faster variant, *passo e mezzo* (step-and-a-half). Pesaro's defense of dancing as a noble art established rules and also required that some dancers perform with professional standards, which displayed their technique for presentation and entertainment.

The study of dance techniques unified the court artists. Masques often featured processional dance suites for couples, where the nobility and their guests could accompany and present a partner to augment their social status. The *pavana* is a slow and dignified dance, usually set to music, and has been compared to the modern day hesitation step used in weddings. In 1581, Fabritio Caroso wrote a book on dance called *Il ballarino*, which describes the selection of a dance partner and courtly etiquette and includes a detailed lesson to practice the combination of steps. Caroso indicated that partnering dances, such as the tarantella and the *basse danse* (low dance), could be attempted by anyone. Other dances were meant for people of particular social classes.

The *basse danse* was a courtly dance for couples that originated in the fourteenth century. Its name is attributed both to its possible origin as a peasant dance and its style of gliding steps in which the feet remain close to the ground. It was performed with various combinations of small bows and a series of walking steps completed by drawing the back foot up to the leading foot. The *basse danse* was typically followed by the stately *pavana*. Finally, the masque would conclude with an after-dance that featured a trained troupe of dancers who would entertain guests with a *galliard*, a combination of four hopping steps and one high leap that permitted the professional dancers to show off their virtuosity.

Catherine de Medici, Queen of France and mother of three French kings, provided her children and their courtiers with rigorous dance training. King Louis XIV, in particular, had a penchant for dance. In 1661, he established the first ballet academy in Paris. Teachers at the academy required dancers to take lessons and be trained in *ballet d'action*, a technique developed by choreographer Jean George Noverre. Noverre's technique produced athletic and artistic professionals who were honored with an appointment and monetary endowment from the French court.

Another book, cleric Thoinot Arbeau's *Orchésographie* (1589), has provided historians with information on ballroom behavior and the interaction between musicians and dancers. Arbeau's entire book was not translated into English until 1961 and is still the only known source for social dances of the time. It includes a male sword dance known as *Les Bouffons*, as well as the Morris Dance, a Northern Highlands–type folk dance. The tarantella is a couple's dance that incorporates man-man and woman-woman partnering, with side-to-side steps, first in a chain and then in two opposing circles, like a wheel. It is characterized by a fast, upbeat tempo, usually 6/8 time (sometimes 4/4), and is accompanied by tambourines. These traditional dances provided a link between court dance and folk dance: elements of folk dance invigorated courtly dances and folk dances utilized movements from courtly dances. The choreography of each form infused the other and class division in dance became less apparent. The main difference between the two forms became less about steps and movements and more about style and elegance.

As early as the fifteenth century, the theatrical stage had been changing and developing to provide a suitable space for new production genres. According to costume historian Regine Mallath, the masques initiated the development of elaborate costume designs made of imported fabrics, exotic feathers, and fur. With the invention of moveable scenery, productions improved technically. King Louis XIV ordered the construction of a stage in the north wing of the Palace of Tuileries in Paris. This *Salle de Machines* housed a stage with overhead rigging that allowed actors in harness—including the King himself—to "fly" in productions based on Greek and Roman mythology. The masques assisted in unifying French culture and presenting the country's ruler publicly in a worldly way. Court masques have been documented as the training ground for talented artists who were involved in singing, acting, and stage design. It is in the court masque that dancers first explored the theatrical art that became the floorshow.

Performing Ensembles in Post-Colonial America

One major component of the floorshow is the size of the cast, referred to as an ensemble. Large groups of performers in synchronized steps and harmonized songs were appealing to audiences, so dancers were seldom presented as soloists in the early incarnations of the floorshow in North America. Beginning in the eighteenth century, passengers and performers began traveling in crude wagons between the cities and towns of the American colonies, first within New England in 1744, then between New York and Philadelphia in 1756.

By the mid nineteenth century, U.S. theatregoers were enjoying traveling-company performances of Shakespearean and other classic European plays, acrobatics, and concert arts with singing, dancing, and comedy routines. But not every town was large or prosperous enough to support a bricks-and-mortar theatre. Towns on the expanding frontier flocked to showboats, specially outfitted steamboats that transported theatrical troupes up and down the major rivers and doubled as theatre buildings. The companies traveling the rivers west of St. Louis (and along the Ohio River, which had two ports dedicated to military transport) performed flamboyant musical shows that depicted familiar American patriotic themes. Between 1850 and 1870, ensembles also traveled by stagecoach to perform at venues such as California's Sacramento Theatre and San Francisco Musical Hall.

Edna Ferber's iconic novel *Show Boat* (1926) tells the story of life on a Mississippi showboat before the Civil War. It was adapted into a musical play, with music by Jerome Kern and lyrics by Oscar Hammerstein II, and has had several motion picture treatments. The *Water Queen* was a major showboat in the late 1880s that featured The Four Bryants, a singing family act. One of the family's daughters wrote that when she was a child, "engagements usually lasted a full summer," but that by the early 1900s, with "the improvement of roads, the rise of the automobile, motion pictures and the maturation of the river culture, showboats had declined in popularity." (Bryant 27)

In the 1830s and early 1840s, a new sort of entertainment, the minstrel show, featuring brief burlesques and comic *entr'actes*, became popular and eventually emerged as a full-fledged performance form. By the next decade, the minstrel show was an

American entertainment form consisting of comic skits, variety acts, dancing, and music. Minstrel shows featured large ensemble casts and were popular at venues in river towns.

Black performers, however, were often subjected to racist attitudes and discrimination, and black ensembles were not permitted to entertain white audiences in many locations. The musical arrangements were especially targeted to appeal to whites. Black characters were typically portrayed by white performers in burnt-cork makeup. There were exceptions, however. William Henry Lane, a notable black tap dance master, was invited to join a whites-only minstrel troupe, but was required at times to wear darker blackface makeup. Minstrelsy declined in popularity in the early twentieth century and by the 1930s was considered a relic of the Civil War era.

Variety theatre had existed before 1860 in Europe and elsewhere and by the turn of the twentieth century it was attracting American audiences with musical revues that featured large ensembles of dancers, singers, and other entertainers. In the early 1880s, New York theatre manager Tony Pastor, a former circus ringmaster, established vaudeville theatre for the middle class. Vaudeville is a theatrical term that loosely describes variety theatre acts suitable for matinée audiences, which appealed to women and children, and evening shows with an exotic edge for men. Also at this time, the Yiddish theatre developed as a uniquely American art form in the Eastern European Jewish immigrant community in New York City and other urban centers. The Yiddish theatre featured stars that went on to the legitimate vaudeville circuit, like George Burns and Gracie Allen, The Marx Brothers, and W.C. Fields.

France

By 1880, the Montmartre district in Paris had become famous for rowdy cabarets and music halls such as the Folies Bergère. Founded in 1869 as the Folies *Trévise*, this venue featured operettas, male and female acrobatic acts with music and oftentimes traveling troupes of tight-rope walkers, clowns, and trained animal acts. Louise Weber, a dancer affectionately known as *la Goulue* (the Glutton), snatched drinks off the tables, performed high kicks and flipped off men's hats with her toe. In 1887, cabarets were licensed and regulated by the city government of Paris, which prescribed safety standards and health measures. In return, they were permitted to offer cocktails and entertainment like traditional theatres.

During the Belle Époque period, (1880–1900), the Moulin Rouge (founded 1889), a cabaret near the Pigalle district of Paris, gained an international reputation. This was where the dance known as the *can-can* originated and the Quat'zarts Ball began. The latter, an annual hazing ritual involving full-body painting by student artists, is still practiced today. The Moulin Rouge became famous for its uncensored shows. Its 1878 striptease *Le Coucher d'Yvette* (1878) (Yvette's Bedroom) featured a woman undressing and bathing on stage. This production first drew aside the curtain between legitimate and salacious theatre. In 1893, The Moulin Rouge transformed *Bal de Quat'zarts* into a production that featured a nude Cleopatra surrounded by a processional of young, naked women. In 1907, the cabaret performer Colette had a lesbian affair with her dance mentor, **Mathilde de Morny, the Marquise de Belbeuf. The two women** capitalized on their fame with a pantomime routine entitled *le Rêve d'Égypte* (The Dream of Egypt) in which they exchanged an onstage kiss. Police reports blamed this lesbian kiss as the cause of a riot that forced the Moulin Rouge to close its doors for renovations.

Over the years, performers' routines were identified by genres that referred to the establishments where they performed. Cabarets catered to the bourgeoisie and cabaret performances tended to be sophisticated, like the audience itself. Music hall entertainment, intended for less well-to-do audiences, was earthier and more spontaneous. The floorshow has links to the cabaret format, which is distinguished by both the genre and the performance venue. A cabaret has tables and chairs, dining, refreshments, and a stage for performances that are usually introduced by a master of ceremonies. The traditional theatre, music hall, and concert saloon (U.S.A.) are defined more by the style of show, the size of the audience, and the concessions offered. In 1899, the Casino de Paris was built as an arena theatre that featured a large stage for various orchestras and space for social dancing. A famous French star of this period, Mistinguett, performed musical numbers with an all-male chorus line dressed in tuxedos. Her signature routine was as a *gommeuse* (eccentric) comic character who flirted with the tourist audience to "come closer." She became well known for singing "Mon Homme" (My Man), in

1916, a torch song later popularized by the American comedienne Fannie Brice in the *Ziegfeld Follies* in 1920. In the early twentieth century, the entertainment road between France and America was a two-way street: Parisian influences became the vogue in the United States and jazz music, vaudeville, and variety acts were exported to Paris and other European destinations.

Germany

By 1901, the German *Kabarett* (cabaret) had created the *Überbrettl* (super-stage) venue, which shared the atmosphere of intimacy with the French cabaret; however, its limited stage space was better suited for comic and small musical performances that attracted lower class audiences. In the 1920s, Berlin had a thriving theatre arts community that rivaled that of Paris. Storefronts and *Wirtshäuser* (inns) were refurbished to accommodate the international tourists and locals doing business in the city. The Jackson Girls were one of many professional dance troupes that performed in cinemas before the movie was screened, five shows per day on the Berlin Cinema-Theatre circuit. Berliners attended the music halls to see motion pictures as a main attraction. The dance revues, presented with orchestral music, were an added bonus.

New York City

By the 1900s, tap dance acts were performing on the vaudeville stages of New York City and were often called in for an olio, a short dance routine or song performed as an encore after the performance of a dramatic play. The growth of the lower-priced cinema and olios in the early 1910s, however, dealt a heavy economic blow to New York's vaudeville theatre circuit.

The American musical revue format featured glamorous girls and catchy show tunes. On Broadway, the most famous of these was the *Ziegfeld Follies*, in which impresario Florenz Ziegfeld imported the Parisian revue concept to Broadway, hoping to appeal to more upscale audiences. His "follies" celebrated beautiful American girls and patriotic music, and his chorus line was a forerunner of precision team dancing troupes such as the Rockettes. The first *Ziegfeld Follies*, an American imitation of a Parisian follies show, *The Parisian Model*, took place in 1907 and starred Anna Held, Ziegfeld's wife. The appeal of this intimate nightclub concept of a star in a show with a large supporting chorus like Mistenguett, from the Casino de Paris, eventually diverged into several different styles of performance, mostly due to the influence of jazz music and musicians from the speakeasies in Chicago during Prohibition. "Floorshow" is a theatrical term from the 1920s. It was a signal by the restaurant manager for the waiters to clear the tables for a show that featured a master of ceremonies/magician and a small line of chorus girls.

The next development in the evolution of the floorshow involved changes in the physical theatre itself. The innovative Mr. Ziegfeld hired Joseph Urban, a theatre technologist, to design a mechanized stage platform that could roll back to reveal a dance floor. The stage could accommodate large moving sets and these, synchronized choreography, and costumes became icons associated with revues. Ziegfeld then added a late-night *Follies Revue* in the New Amsterdam Theater's rooftop theatre area. The roof itself was a stage platform that rolled back to reveal the girls scandalously posed overhead. Stagecraft innovations were expressions of engineers and technicians in collaboration that would enhance choreography of dancers to an art form. Costumes were identified with the performers in story scenarios. In 1911, Jesse Louis Lasky, later the founder of Paramount Pictures, produced two Broadway musicals, *Hello, Paris* and *À la Broadway*. These revues were presented in a multi-act show format that combined music,

dance, skits, and the frank display of the female body. Though the revue has its roots in nineteenth-century American popular entertainment, the format grew into a substantial cultural presence of its own between 1916 and 1932.

The Movies from Hollywood, California

During the 1920s, Busby Berkeley, a dance director for many Broadway musicals, developed his style of choreography into a signature trademark. Berkeley's dance sequences featured a large cast of female dancers with costumes and props. When he relocated to Hollywood, Berkeley became a movie director and was given the freedom to develop extravagant aerial cinematography for the film studios which involved complex geometric patterns of choreography. His overhead point of view began to define dancers' roles in musical revues and was the centerpiece of the theatrical effects in his movies, such as *Gold Diggers of 1933, 1935*, and *1937*. In *Dames* (1934), everything moved, including the sets and the stage. These segments were captured on film through a camera mounted on top of a modified crane nicknamed the "flying trapeze."

World War II through Today

When the Second World War began, Paris's Folies Bergère, Casino de Paris, and Chantilly Theatre remained open. The Jackson Girls had been booked to perform in the Folies Bergère, but were sent back to Berlin because the performers were mostly Germans. During the German Occupation of Paris (1942–1944), theatres that stayed open had to hire performers who would play to Nazi officers and sympathizers in the audience. One dancer named Bluebell was a native of Ireland, a neutral nation, and decided to stay on as a member of the Folies Bergère chorus. When she married a Jewish co-worker, musician and composer Marcel Liebowicz, both were fired and evicted from their apartment in the city. The Nazis were relocating persons of Jewish descent and their spouses, whom they deemed "inferior." After months in safe houses outside Paris, Bluebell began to look for work. Frederic Apcar had been a chorus dancer at the Folies Bergère and knew Bluebell there before the war. Apcar later became the manager of the Chantilly Theatre. The Chantilly provided a space for social dancing and musical entertainment, but it was managed by members of the French Resistance and used as a front for the Allies. It was there that Bluebell managed to maintain a small troupe of her own chorus dancers, aptly named the Bluebells. As she described it, the theatre was "a small, seedy, cabaret that had an underground, black market that was open for services in the lobby." (Perry 156)

After the war, Parisians rejected some theatrical venues because of their association with Nazi sympathizers. Even the management of the *Folies Bergère* was removed from its positions by the postwar regime. Once it was no longer needed for nationalistic purposes, the Chantilly Theatre faded into obscurity.

Welcome to Fabulous Las Vegas Sign. The famous sign was designed by Betty Whitehead Willis. Photography provided by Las Vegas News Bureau, 1963.

Circa 1950s – Las Vegas Strip – This photograph was taken from the top of the Thunderbird Resort facing north. The El Rancho Hotel and Sahara Hotel are shown. Photograph provided by the Las Vegas News Bureau, 1956.

Pictured, Showgirl in rehearsal in the Lido de Paris show- second edition at the Stardust Hotel.

Photography by Jerry Abbott, Joe Buck/courtesy of the Las Vegas News Bureau, 1959.

Pictured, Showgirls and Dancers in the Lido de Paris show at the Stardust Hotel. In front of the "piscine" pool – the scene depicts The Roman Bath. Photo features Valda Boyne (Valda Esau), and Penny Parfit, Bluebell dancers from Paris. Photo provided by the Las Vegas News Bureau, 1958.

Pictured, Showgirls in the Lido de Paris show at the Stardust Hotel. Photography by Jerry Abbott, Joe Buck/courtesy of the Las Vegas News Bureau, 1959.

Pictured, Showgirl in the Lido de Paris show - second edition at the Stardust Hotel. Photo courtesy of the Las Vegas News Bureau, 1959.

Pictured, Showgirls and the Cast of the Lido de Paris show rehearsal– Second Edition at the Stardust Hotel. Photography by Jerry Abbott, Joe Buck / courtesy of the Las Vegas News Bureau, 1959.

Pictured, The Bluebells and Showgirls in the Lido de Paris show – Second Edition at the Stardust Hotel.

Photography by Jerry Abbott/Joe Buck, courtesy of the Las Vegas News Bureau, 1959.

CHAPTER II

AN OVERVIEW OF THE STRUCTURE OF FLOORSHOWS

Paris

In 1945, on the Champs-Élysées in Paris, an old movie palace was transformed into a theatre-restaurant concept called the Lido de Paris. The first show, *Sans rimes, ni raisons* (1946) (Without Rhyme or Reason) featured the Bluebell girls, the Kelly boys, and the most famous innovation, Madame Bluebell's introduction of the super-tall topless dancer. The Lido's creative team included Donn Arden, an American choreographer from St. Louis, Missouri, who created the shows; Pierre-Louis Guerin, who as artistic director designed the Lido's interior; and Renée Fraday, a former dancer turned stage engineer, who installed hydraulic lifts for the enormous sets. The Lido de Paris set the standards for performers in floorshows and established the genre as a theatrical art.

Las Vegas

In the 1930s, Highway 91, otherwise known as the Las Vegas Strip, featured rodeo complexes. Nevada was the first U.S. state to legalize gambling. By the time the Lido de Paris opened at the Stardust Casino and Hotel in 1958, the notoriety of the French floorshows' topless showgirls had already launched many imitators imported from Paris. By 1959, the Folies Bergère had opened at the Tropicana Casino Hotel, and the following year, the Moulin Rouge show premiered at the Las Vegas Hilton Casino Hotel. Donn Arden secured the exclusive use of the Stardust's Café Continental showroom for the Lido de Paris for 33 years and established the floorshow as the theatrical art of Las Vegas. (Figure 1)

The Café Continental Showroom at the Stardust Hotel and Casino was designed as a theatrical experience that became synonymous with the casino-hotels and all other floorshows on the Las Vegas Strip. The tuxedoed house manager made a patron list from the casino game floor about an hour before each show and admitted VIPs one by one past a red velvet rope. The showroom had table seating for

1,200 patrons, which was served by a five-star culinary and uniformed hospitality staff for the dinner show and cocktail service during intermissions. (Figure 2)

The entire stage and backstage were on elevated platforms that could be lowered into position. The stage floor was divided into three separate risers that permitted the stagehands to switch out set pieces between scenes, allowing transitions to be executed smoothly and safely while raising performers into position in seconds after wardrobe changes.

The Las Vegas showrooms were structurally modified to fit within the hotel and casino environment. The Café Continental showroom was installed with the latest technology and had a *pasarela*, an extended runway designed to let the performers step off of the main stage. (Illustration 1) The interior had terrace-style seating with panoramic views and a kings' row with comfortable red leather booths around the outside of the *pasarela*. (Figure 3)

The Backstage Door

The stage manager was responsible for the performers' arrivals and departures. Only performers with authorized identification were permitted entry through the stage

Figure 1 The Rocket Girls at the Grand Opening of the Stardust Hotel and Casino. Photo courtesy of the Las Vegas News Bureau 1958.

Figure 2 The Stardust Hotel and Casino Marquee 1958. Photograph from the Las Vegas News Bureau.

door from the parking lot at the rear of the hotel. The backstage crew comprised stagehands, technicians, and wardrobe dressers who assisted the performers in their stage exits and entrances on a cue light. The sets included rolling grand staircases, an ice rink, a waterfall, and animal cages for elephants and tigers, and were pre-positioned backstage and secured 30 feet below stage.

Figure 3 Café Continental Showroom at the Stardust Hotel and Casino. Photograph courtesy of the Las Vegas News Bureau 1971.

Figure 4 The Bluebells arrive under security in 1958. Photo courtesy from the Las Vegas News Bureau.

Figure 5 The Bluebells, Donn Arden, Bluebell, and Mayor of Las Vegas in 1958. Photo from the Las Vegas News Bureau.

In 1961, the *Las Vegas Review Journal* reported that the Dunes Hotel and Casino was struggling to attract patrons. The Dunes had a main stage for star headliners, but its size was too small for a floorshow with a large ensemble of dancers in big headdresses and costumes. After an appearance on *The Ed Sullivan Variety Show* in 1955 with the cast of *Ballet Parisien*, Frederic Apcar approached the Dunes' management with a floorshow concept for the Persian Lounge that could showcase French singers, dancers, and international guest stars. Apcar's *Vive Les Girls* "was the first lounge-sized revue which featured a cast of 30 dancers, daring choreography, barely any costuming, and performances as late as 3 a.m.," according to the *Review-Journal*'s entertainment columnist, Mike Weatherford. The lounge-sized format launched a floorshow revolution—a late-late-night floorshow. In 1963, the Dunes's management had the confidence to invest $2 million in a new showroom with the premiere of Apcar's *Casino de Paris*, which featured a 100-member cast and singer Line Renaud, who had starred in the original French production of the same name.

By the 1970s, the Las Vegas floorshow formula was a success again and was produced many times at other preeminent hotels such as the Sands Casino Hotel (*The Copa Girls*) and the Sahara Casino Hotel (*Sahara Girls*). Hollywood movie stars took part, including Marlene Dietrich in the Lido de Paris' *Le Revue Bravo* (1949); Shirley MacLaine was even hired to perform routines in 1977's *Allez Lido*. According to the Las Vegas Tourism Authority reports, in 1972, the showroom productions were setting attendance records and audiences were coming to Las Vegas from Los Angeles to see the Parisian shows and not just for the table games.

Atlantic City

In 1979, the casino-hotels in Atlantic City wanted to repeat the success that had attracted audiences to Las Vegas. One of the shows, *Steppin' Out* (1981) at Harrah's Marina Hotel and Casino, was a musical revue reminiscent of the lavish French productions of the 1920s. *Steppin' Out* was staged and choreographed by Ron Lewis and featured an ensemble of 18 dancers who performed scenes depicting the can-can, a tropical nightclub, and a modern dance–style Aztec ritual. (Figure 6) The Las Vegas floorshow formula was a success in Paris and Las Vegas, but in the casino-hotels of Atlantic City, there was one major artistic exception: no nude dancers or topless performers were permitted in the floorshows by civil code. Since the Atlantic City floorshows were censored, they never reached the same level of success as the Las Vegas shows and they were eventually replaced by variety acts, civic events, and rock concerts.

(Figure 7)

Figure 7 The Ron Lewis Dancers in the *Aztec Ritual* in Frederic Apcar's Steppin' Out at Harrah's Marina Hotel in Atlantic City, New Jersey, 1981. Photo courtesy of Frederic Apcar Productions.

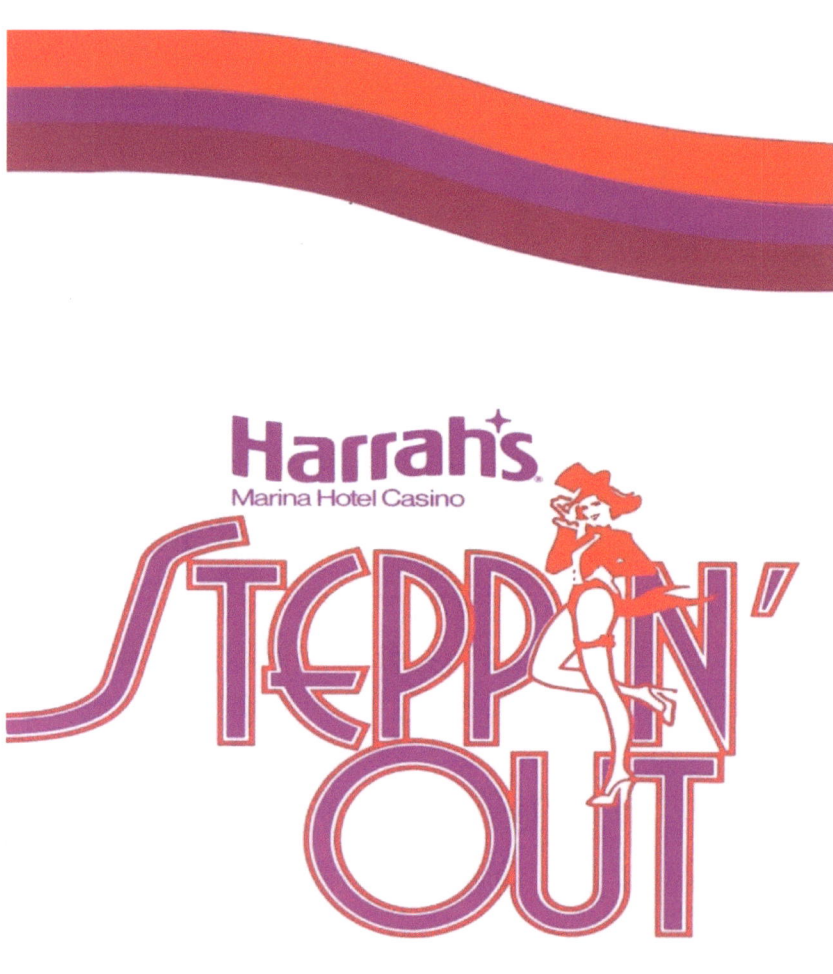

Figure 8 Steppin' Out show program from Harrah's Marina Hotel Casino, 1981.

Pictured, Showgirl in the Lido de Paris show '66 – rehearsal at the Stardust Hotel. Photography by Cook & English. Courtesy of the Las Vegas News Bureau, 1965.

Pictured, Showgirl from the Lido de Paris show '66 in rehearsal at the Stardust Hotel. Photography by Cook & English. Courtesy of the Las Vegas News Bureau, 1965.

Pictured, Showgirl Elaine Juliano in the Lido de Paris show 1966 - backstage at the Stardust Hotel.

Photo courtesy of the Las Vegas News Bureau, 1966.

Pictured, Showgirls in dress rehearsal for the Lido de Paris show '66 at the Stardust Hotel. Photography by Cook & English. Courtesy of the Las Vegas News Bureau, 1965.

Pictured, The Bluebells in the Lido de Paris show '66 at the Stardust Hotel. Photography by Cook & English, 1965. Photo courtesy of the Las Vegas News Bureau.

Pictured, Showgirls from The Lido de Paris Show '66 at the Stardust Hotel. Photography by Cook & English, 1965. Photo courtesy of the Las Vegas News Bureau.

Pictured, Showgirls in the Lido de Paris show at the Stardust Hotel. Photo courtesy of the Las Vegas News Bureau, 1968.

Pictured, Showgirls in the Lido de Paris show at the Stardust Hotel. Opening number.

Photo by Wolf Wergin/Las Vegas News Bureau, 1968.

Pictured, Showgirl in the Lido de Paris at the Stardust Hotel. Photo courtesy of the Las Vegas News Bureau, 1968.

The Las Vegas Strip. Aerial image taken from the top of the Dunes Hotel and features marquees. Photo provided by the Las Vegas News Bureau, 1967.

Photo, The Las Vegas Strip with the Stardust Hotel marquee. Courtesy of the Las Vegas News Bureau, 1967.

CHAPTER III

THE LAS VEGAS PRODUCTION OF A FLOORSHOW

The Lido de Paris's American-style interpretation of a French entertainment form would establish the floorshow as the theatrical art of Las Vegas. Its combination of cabaret style and stage effects has been emulated internationally and set professional standards for working dancers. (Figure 9) The author of this thesis was a member of the cast of *Allez Lido* from 1978 to 1981. This eight-act floorshow featured an ensemble of 32 Bluebells, 8 Lido boys, 20 showgirls, a comic juggler, and a magic act with trained animals from Asia and Africa. The chapter that follows describes all the elements that went into creating this elaborate spectacle.

The casino recruited dancers trained in disciplines of ballet, jazz, and modern dance from Sadler's Wells Dance Theatre, London's School of the Royal Ballet, and associated dance studios in Paris, London, and Las Vegas (joined occasionally by a newcomer discovered by one of Madame Bluebell's talent scouts). The auditions took place backstage at the theatre where dancers were interviewed and put through their paces. The floorshow style of dance is athletic and requires physical endurance for three weeks of rehearsals lasting up to 12 hours per day. The physical requirements were rigid. The age range for both male and female dancers was 16–34 years, with height measurements of 5'10" - 6' 2". After the initial interview with the company managers, dancers were asked to submit a photograph and résumé, and received a number on a sheet of paper that was fastened to their attire. The combinations of steps were then demonstrated by dance captains who would assess how quickly and accurately each potential new hire could acquire the steps and be ready to start. (Figure 10)

The Lido de Paris offered salaried contracts for six months, travel, advancement, and foreign worker visas to permit British, Australian, and French performers to work in the United States. Foreign and American performers were often employed when they were under the legal age of 21. It was illegal for them to be seen in the casino where alcoholic beverages were served. Dancers could be hired as young as 16, which required the stage manager to assume their supervisory guardianship. If minor performers were ever absent due to illness or injury, the manager was required to follow a specific set of state and federal laws. Immigration and Naturalization officials (INS) had the power to detain and deport foreign performers within 72 hours should laws protecting minors be breached. Underage American performers who were not emancipated were remanded to their parent or guardian after the show.

The Lido de Paris show was presented twice nightly, and a third show was added on Saturdays at 4 p.m. The early show at 7 p.m. included dinner and the late show at 11 p.m. included cocktails and dessert. Performers were often contracted with an understudy, a replacement performer of equal caliber who stood by in case of injury or took over during the performer's vacation. Once dancers were under contract, it precluded them from participating in a sport or activity that could cause physical harm. The cast was informed of set changes and guest-act substitutions that would require placement rehearsals after the last show each day. The reason for these extra rehearsals was primarily for safety because performers often would not recognize each other without their onstage makeup and elaborate costumes. (Figure 11) Placement rehearsals started at 1:00 a.m. Depending on the number of replacements, it could last for a couple of hours.

Figure 9 Lido de Paris Program from the Stardust Hotel and Casino in 1977. Photo courtesy of Boyd Gaming.

Figure 10 Bluebell dancer auditions. Photo from the Las Vegas News Bureau.

The Lido de Paris's *Allez Lido*

Act One: *Paris Toujours*! (Be Mine) *Toujours Lido!* As the house lights dimmed over the audience in the showroom, a quick musical scale and a drum roll from the timpani section struck a downbeat, and signaled to the house manager to settle the wait staff. The Lido de Paris orchestra conductor raised his baton for the lights in the showroom to dim. The overture's rhythm section accompanied the motion of the follow-spotlight as it tracked back and forth above them. Suddenly, three showgirls descended from the ceiling on a disk platform suspended by cable wires. As they stepped off the disk, they moved in collective rhythm upstage (away from the audience) while another music cue signaled the cast procession. (Figure 10)

Figure 11 Lido de Paris' Dancer Rehearsals.

Act One celebrated the American musical. The music motif was romantic, with songs by George Gershwin, including "Rhapsody in Blue," "Our Love Is Here to Stay," and "Love Walked In." The dancers, singers, and showgirls were stationed in pre-set positions backstage. A stagehand signaled for a section of the stage that would elevate the grand staircase set. Downstage, facing the audience, the cast made its entrance. First, the male dancers stepped on to the *pasarela*. (Figure 12) Each dancer's step out was synchronized to the parting showroom curtain. The male dancers were pre-positioned in the wings and entered from opposite sides, first meeting two by two, and then splitting off at center stage. Each male dancer had an introduction accompanied by a musical note; the Lido boys tipped their hat to the audience with one hand and leaped forward in combinations of high jumps, knee-spins, and pirouette turns to emphasize their costumes. Their first outfit was a cape made of white linen fabric with blue satin lining, a high starched collar, a vested jump-suit, a custom silk shirt with rhinestone-studded French cuffs, a top hat, gloves, and white ankle-high boots.

(Illustration 2)

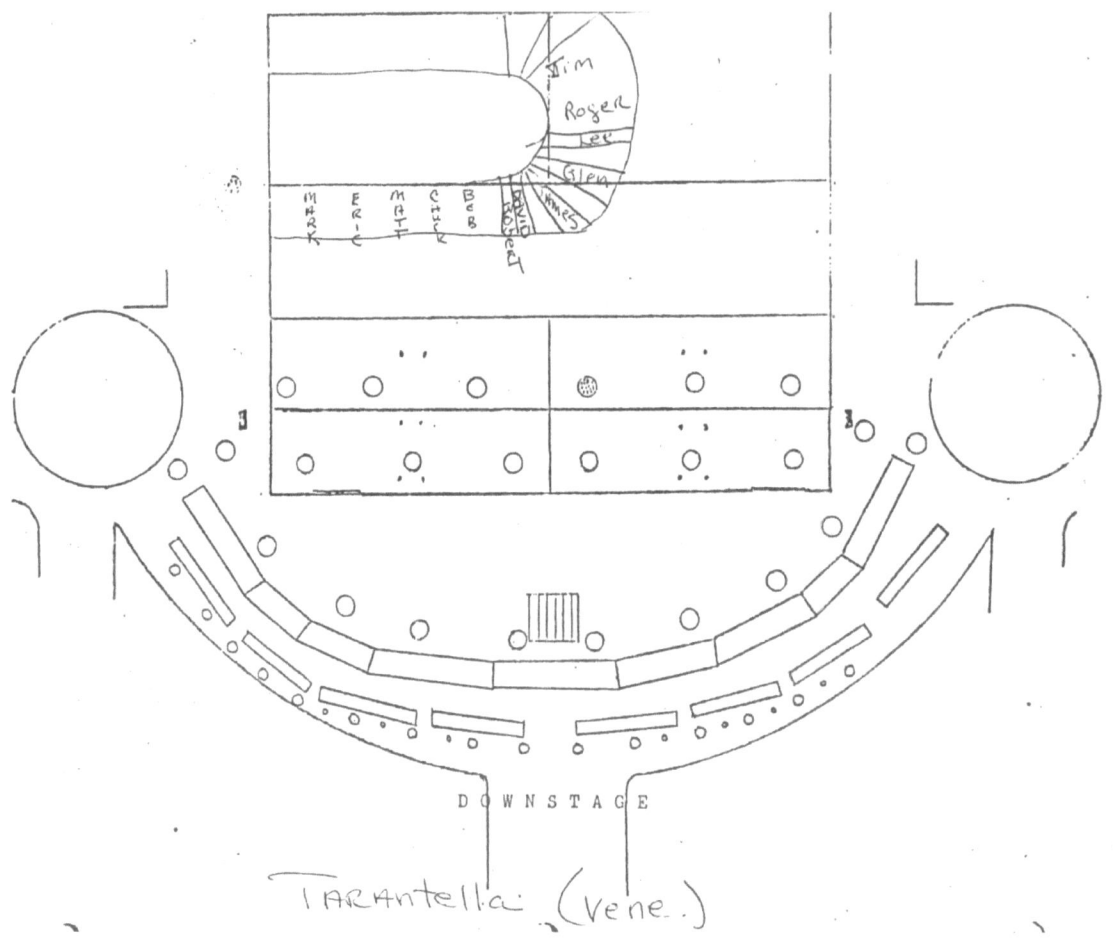

Illustration 2 Venetian Tarantella floor plan for staging the production number.

The Bluebells then entered from opposite sides of the stage carrying large blue-and-white peacock-feather fans. In a fast-moving processional, they turned on the stage apron as an ensemble, opening their fans to form a giant bloom. The Bluebells wore identical full length silver gowns with rhinestone tiaras and jeweled accessories. As they strutted on the *pasarela*, the Bluebells revealed the topless showgirls, whose costumes, designed by Folco of Paris, were styled with white mink fur pelts trimmed with blue peacock feathers, a rhinestone G-string, and an elaborate headdress known as frontage. Posed within an arm's length of the audience on the *pasarela*, they sauntered with a hesitation-step onto the main stage, followed by the Bluebells. At the end of the opening number, the Lido Male Dancers followed in formation behind the Bluebells for the close of the opening act curtain. (Figure 13)

Pictured, Bluebell, Miranda Coe in silver gown, with blue and white feather plumage fans. In arabesque, 1980.

Act Two featured Kris Kremo, a juggling act. The performer would begin simply by juggling three bricks, then six vases, then six fire-burning batons, with musical accompaniment. He juggled just about anything, while encouraging audience participation and beverage service. Meanwhile, behind the main curtain, the sets were secured in place and dancers were dressed in layers of costumes, called pre-sets. These allowed for different roles to be performed with split-second costume changes.

Act Three: *Les Amours de Casanova* began with a classical music chord from a harpsichord. As the curtain opened, a male principal dancer portrayed Casanova in his legendary amorous affairs. In sequences of choreography that involved the moving-set, a two-sided circular platform turned from the scene of a masquerade ball to Casanova's secret bedroom chamber set. During the masquerade, the focus shifted from a *pas de deux* (duet) already in progress between a showgirl and Casanova to a *ménage a trois* (collection of three) as another showgirl entered the bedroom set through a secret door.

Figure 13 Lido de Paris, *Allez Lido* at the Stardust Hotel in 1978. Photograph from the Las Vegas News Bureau.

Pictured, Showgirl Barbara Beverly in a Herma Voss designed rhinestone studded head-dress. It has a necklace attached to the bottom of the seat and a silver link chain hooked the collar in place. The arching fox fur piece was also trimmed with blue feathers, complete with a rhinestone jeweled hat. She is surrounded by blue and white plumage fans that the Bluebells held in position.

The sets were positioned to incorporate a seamless display of women of the court, as the "living curtain." Showgirls were seamlessly placed on a grand staircase as statuesque, fashionable nudes with high, powdered coiffure wigs with feather plumes. The masquerade gowns were break-away costumes, some pale blue satin with tight-fitting bodices and some low-cut, rose colored gowns with satin robes in blue, a stomacher, hooped-petticoat, attached leg-of-mutton sleeves, a rhinestone chastity belt and high-heeled shoes.

The set pieces moving into place disguised Casanova's bedroom chamber. The dancers who portrayed the masquerade guests were repositioned on the moving set. The climax of the scene exposed the showgirls who were making a quick exit. The hoops of the gowns of the living curtain that made up the padded bedroom wall were left as empty harnesses. The scene ended with Casanova left alone, chained onto the bed. A scenic backdrop depicting a Venetian canal redirected the focus to an ensemble of male dancers and Bluebells dressed as Italian villagers in a celebration of the tarantella dance.

Act Four: *The Ice Fantasy* featured Nikki and Robbie, champion figure skaters, in an act on ice. One of their most exciting moves was when Robbie pushed the small of Nikki's back while lifting her above his head. She opened her legs and arms into a starburst position while he spun below her. As soon as he could attain the proper velocity, he sent her soaring into a move called a death-drop. The male skater positions the woman's hips from the starburst, collapses her limbs into a straight line, and grabs her ankles, swinging her face inches from the ice, then slowly reduces his spin motion, while she collapses herself into his arms. The stagecraft effects of dry ice formed misty clouds that were subdued in the sunken footlights with hues of pink and blue. Nikki and Robbie did their routine twice nightly and three times on Saturday for 20 years. The death-drop was their signature move and the choreography came to represent the Stardust's galactic theme of soaring through space. For their encore, a stagehand signaled their platform to descend and remove the ice rink for the next scene. All the while Nikki and

Robbie continued spinning. The audience was left gasping. (Figure 14)

Figure 14 Ice Fantasy. Champion Figure Skaters were raised and lowered by stage elevators into view from a moveable ice rink. The ice rink was placed in front of the main showroom curtain. Lido de Paris at the Stardust Hotel. 1975. Photography from the Las Vegas News Bureau.

Act Five: *Africa! Africa!* As the act curtain opened, the stage was dark. Drum beats accompanied two African elephants and their handlers as they walked on stage. On the *pasarela*, they turned and strolled onto the set of the Village of Ketchell. The legend of the village was represented by 3 female dancers who would perform an exotic tribal dance as the gates to the temple would open. The elephants would make their way through the cast, while the entire ensemble then portrayed tourists on safari or African natives. Performing on cue, the elephants would become startled and "stampeded" offstage led by their handlers. A multitude of lights would blast the stage, portraying a volcano erupting. Threatened by imminent danger, the natives and tourists had to run down ramps with fire sticks and exit as sacrificial souls. When, suddenly, the stage ascended into a 30-foot waterfall with a drop that went into a pool in the showroom's basement. The village set is left destroyed, leaving a cliff on stage, a few native dressed dancers. With the waterfall still purging and running, the showroom lights would go dark. Then, there would be the three female dancers, at the base of the waterfall, as the orchestra would crescendo into a loud horrific note. (Figure 15)

Figure 15 Dancers at the Lido de Paris, Stardust Hotel, *Africa! Africa!* Pictured is the Water fall that was designed on elevators that were raised up by hydraulic lifts. The waterfall is on the main stage. The scene featured the ensemble of dancers positioned on the edge of the drain pool and the pasarela. Photography from the Las Vegas News Bureau.

Figure 16 The Stardust Casino and Hotel Marquee with Siegfried and Roy at the Lido de Paris. Photography from the Las Vegas News Bureau, 1981.

Act Six: Siegfried and Roy became star magicians and illusionists in Las Vegas, where audiences enthusiastically embraced them and their Siberian white tigers. Their act featured feats of illusion such as sawing a female assistant in half and making an elephant disappear. A spinning mirrored globe was attached to a crane holding a tiger. The tiger appeared on one side of the stage in a cage, while, spinning on a crane above the audience, Roy disappeared in the dark. Siegfried ended up in a spotlight, where he found two white tiger cubs. Running downstage, dangerously towards the audience, Siegfried would freeze in position on the *pasarela* as the female tiger called to her white cubs to unite. (Figure 16)

Act Seven: *Chez Maxim* featured the Lido boys singing French songs about some of the famous neighborhoods in Paris. The scenic backdrops depicted scenes from Paris with landmarks such the Arc de Triomphe and the Latin Quarter, where the performers portrayed painters costumed in capes and berets. The stage action transitioned from the strolling singers to the Rue Royale, where bistro waiters engaged in a comic routine of male bravado competing for restaurant patrons. Two groups of male dancers formed opposing lines, balancing drink trays strapped to their wrists. The scene featured a precision, floor-sweeping, Russian Cossack dance, where the male dance ensemble linked arms in a forward motion knee slide. As the production number came to a close, the ensemble would stop on the edge of the stage inches from the audience. During the applause, the scene transitioned into one representing the streets of Pigalle. The male singers entered from the wings and sang a medley of songs about unrequited love, as the stage lights dimmed to a soft, romantic glow.

Act Eight: *Gran Prix Je t'aime* was the finale of *Allez Lido!* and featured an illuminated tribute to the City of Light. As the entire cast descended from an enormous white staircase that led to the stage, thousands of lights illuminated the stair steps to synchronized music. The male dancers were dressed in black velvet tuxedos with gold shirts, black bowties, and ankle high black boots, as they revealed a sparkling outline of the Eiffel Tower in lights. As the main stage curtain closed, the entire cast sang, *"Bonsoir A Bientot, Allez Lido!"* to resounding applause. (Illustration 3)

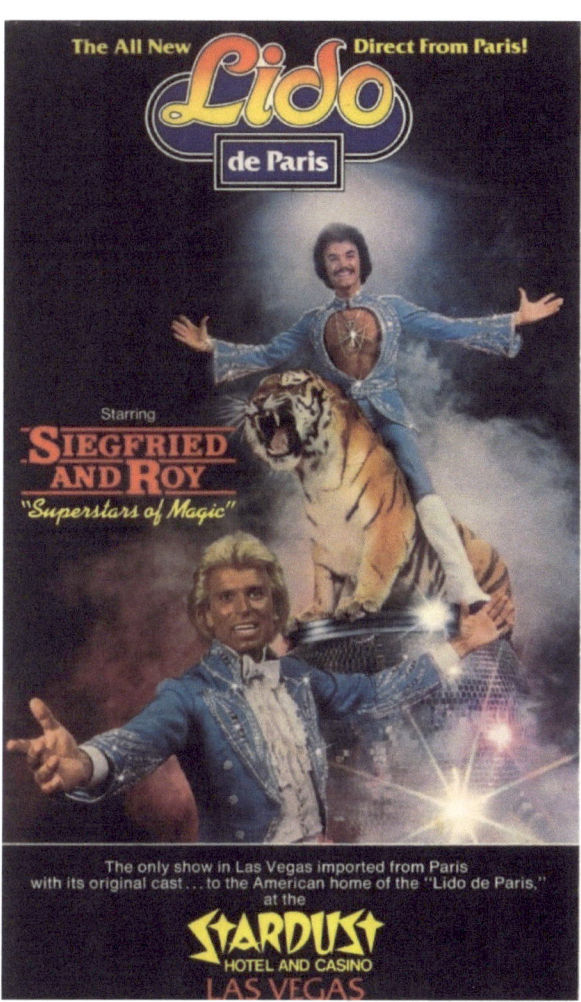

Figure 17 Lido de Paris Program. The Stardust Hotel and Casino, Siegfried and Roy 1980.

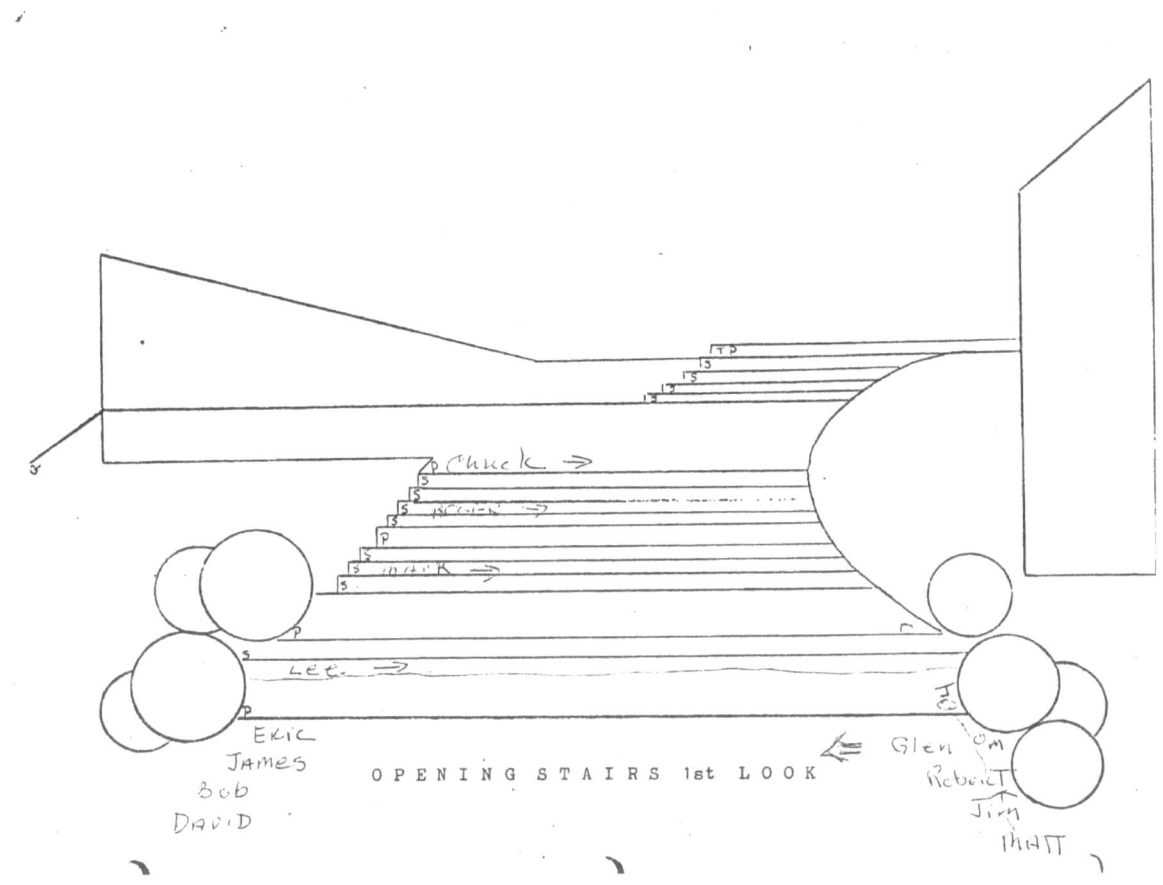

Illustration 3 Indicates the Male Dancers placement floor plan drawn with pedestals. Stardust Hotel Showroom stage from the Lido de Paris' Allez Lido 1978.

The Lido de Paris at the Stardust Hotel. Photo courtesy of the Las Vegas News Bureau, 1984.

The Bluebells wore silver, beaded rhinestone gowns, that were cut at the waist with an open mid-drift, brassiere. The head dress with a cut rhinestone-studded tiara, was accessorized with silver beaded bicep bands and silver character shoes.

Pictured, Showgirls, The Lido de Paris' *Bonjour la Nuit* show at the Stardust Hotel. Photo courtesy of the Las Vegas News Bureau, 1972.

Pictured, The Bluebells in the Lido de Paris show at the Stardust Hotel. Photography by Lee & English, courtesy of the Las Vegas News Bureau, 1975.

Pictured, Showgirl from the Lido de Paris at the Stardust Hotel. Photo courtesy of the Las Vegas News Bureau, 1972.

THE FLOORSHOW

Pictured, Showgirls, and costumed Knights on horses in the Lido de Paris show at the Stardust Hotel.

Photo courtesy of the Las Vegas News Bureau, 1972.

Pictured, The Lido de Paris show at the Stardust Hotel. Photo courtesy of the Las Vegas News Bureau, 1975.

Pictured, The Bluebells in the Lido de Paris show at the Stardust Hotel. Photography by Lee & English. Courtesy of the Las Vegas News Bureau, 1975.

Pictured, Showgirls and Lido Dancers in the Lido de Paris show, at the Stardust Hotel. Photo by Lee & English, courtesy of the Las Vegas News Bureau, 1975.

Pictured, Dancers - Bluebells in the Lido de Paris at the Stardust Hotel.

Photo by Lee & English, courtesy of the Las Vegas News Bureau, 1975.

Pictured, The Bluebells in the Lido de Paris *Rio* show at the Stardust Hotel. Photo courtesy of the Las Vegas News Bureau, 1975.

Pictured, Showgirls in the Lido de Paris show at the Stardust Hotel. Photograph by Lee & English, courtesy of the Las Vegas News Bureau, 1975.

The Bluebells, and Lido Boy Dancers in the Lido de Paris' *Allez Lido* show's "Grand Finale," at the Stardust Hotel. Photo courtesy of the Las Vegas News Bureau, 1980.

Pictured, The Cast of the Lido de Paris' *Allez Lido*, at the Stardust Hotel, 1978. Photo provided by the Las Vegas News Bureau, 1978.

The Strip, photo courtesy of the Las Vegas News Bureau, 1975.

Pictured, Showgirl, Barbara Beverly in the Lido de Paris' *Allez Lido* show at the Stardust Hotel. Photo courtesy of the Las Vegas News Bureau, 1980.

Pictured, the cast of the Lido de Paris' *Allez Lido* show in the Grand Finale number at the Stardust Hotel. Photo courtesy of the Las Vegas News Bureau, 1984.

Pictured, Bluebell, Miranda Coe, in a silver gown embedded with rhinestones and sequins. The opening number costume is accessorized with fans made of blue and white plumage feathers.

The Bluebells entered the stage from both wings to form the famous patterns in precision lines.

Pictured, Bluebell, Miranda Coe, backstage in the dressing room at the Stardust Hotel, 1980.

Backstage in the Stardust Hotel Dressing Room, a Bluebell prepares, 1980.

Pictured, Lido de Paris Dancer, Miranda Coe, at the Stardust Hotel, 1979. Showtime!

Photo details the tiara worn by the Bluebells in the Lido de Paris' *Allez Lido* show at the Stardust Hotel. The full costume was designed for the Bluebell's to perform their famous fan dance, the opening number to the song "Rhapsody in Blue." The silver tiara is embedded with cut rhinestones, with an added accent of dangling tear-drop crystal stones in place of earrings – for a quick change costume design, 1979.

Precision Dance Lines

The Bluebells

The Bluebells costumed in silver gowns with fans made of black and white plumage feathers.

Pictured, dancer, Miranda Coe.

Pictured, The Bluebell Dancers in the Grand Finale, in the Lido de Paris' *Allez Lido* show at the Stardust Hotel, 1979.

Poster Art and Program from the Lido de Paris, in Paris, France.

Pictured, Showgirl, Barbara Beverly on the Program Cover from the Lido de Paris' *Allez Lido* show at the Stardust Hotel, 1979.

Photo of the cast of *Steppin' Out* in the "Tropical Enchantment" production number at Harrah's Hotel in Atlantic City, New Jersey, 1981. Photo courtesy of Frederic Apcar Productions.

The cast of 32 dancers linked arms and through a synchronization forward motion, Ron Lewis' choreography had a syncopated, hitch-step that would propel the line toward the audience, onto the lip of the stage's edge, stopping inches from going over into the pit and audience. It brought the house down.

Pictured, Dancers, (L-R) Victor Culver and Doug Woods in tuxedos for the "Grand Finale," in *Steppin' Out* at Harrah's Hotel in Atlantic City, New Jersey, 1981. Photo courtesy of Frederic Apcar Productions.

THE FLOORSHOW

Cast Photos on the grand staircase in the "Grand Finale" from *Steppin' Out* at Harrah's Marina Hotel in Atlantic City, New Jersey, 1981.

Photo of dancers in the "Tropical Enchantment" number, *Steppin' Out*, Harrah's Marina Hotel, 1981.

Cast photos in the "Aztec Ritual" in Frederic Apcar's *Steppin' Out*. The Aztec costumes had feather brown, white, and black plumage, beaded chest plates, and leather sandals. The stage set is designed as a pyramid with ramp-ways. Costumes conceived and designed by Jose Luis Vinas.

"The French Can Can," in Frederic Apcar's *Steppin Out*. Staged and Choreographed by Ron Lewis.

Cast photos of the "French Can Can" in *Steppin' Out!,* 1981.

The female dancers costumes were designed with a bright red and black glossy color scheme. Designed as a quick change outfit, the skirt was cut as a knee length, full-fit. And featured a multi-layered traditional petti coat with a red-lacy under panty made of a durable chiffon fabric, that contrasted against black fishnet hosiery. The female dancers costume was also accessorized with high button character shoes, white spats, and a red feather plumage headdress, mounted on a black velvet pill-box hat with a chin strap.

Pictured, Dancers, Kathy Degennaro, Doug Woods, and Paula Morman on the white staircase in the "French Can-Can," in *Steppin' Out* (1981).

The male dancers costumes were made of a stretchable and durable red fabric, designed into a jump suit with suspenders, that securely held the red and black striped table waiter uniform which was accessorized with black character boots, white spats, and a black derby hat.

Review from Ocean County Times Observer, Atlantic City, New Jersey, 1981.

Pictured, (Lower L-R) Michael Hackett, Gary Coburn (principal), and Doug Woods, in the "French Can Can" in *Steppin Out, 1981.* The finale of the "French Can Can" linked 9 male dancers in a twisting knee jump.

Cast Photo of the Ron Lewis Dancers – (L-R) Leah Corley, Victoria Petti, Doug Woods, Glenn Nash, Chelsea Field, and Michael Hackett in the "Grand Finale" in *Steppin' Out*, at Harrah's Marina Hotel, 1981. Photo courtesy of Frederic Apcar Productions.

CHAPTER IV

THE FUTURE OF THE FLOORSHOW

The floorshow is a theatrical art whose styles of dance, music, and scenic design reflect the changes to traditional theatre. By the late 1880s, cabarets in Paris were licensed and regulated by code which prescribed safety standards. In return, the cabarets were like theatres in that they were permitted to offer cocktails, and the physical appearance of female performers was developed as the main attraction.

The origins of the floorshow in the Italian and French courts along with the Parisian influence on American musical revues helped establish the floorshow's focus on the dancer. Throughout the years, the showrooms have featured many different kinds of performers. Currently, however, the combination of showy choreography and spectacular staging of large ensemble casts is often received by patrons as kitschy and has been relegated to smaller venues.

Historically, the floorshow reflected a combination of patriotic pride and entertaining vignettes. The floorshow in Las Vegas made the showroom and the floorshow synonymous with Las Vegas entertainment and it was the *Lido de Paris's* American-style interpretation of a classic French entertainment form that became the epitome of this theatrical art form. The combination of cabaret style, topless dancers, and spectacular stage effects has been emulated internationally and set professional standards for working dancers.

In writing this thesis, I discovered that the producer that I worked with in 1981, Frederic Apcar, is truly a show business legend. Further research into the careers and contributions of these pioneers of global entertainment forms, like Apcar, Bluebell, and Arden, could yield fascinating perspectives on the evolution of public taste and the effects of the economy on show business.

In 1977, the original French Lido de Paris was remodeled with panoramic seating for 1,150 patrons. The new suspended audience floor allows the orchestra section to sink below the stage where 300 additional patrons dine. The backstage was modified and expanded to accommodate extra-large sets, such as a replica of a Russian Czar's Palace, live African elephants, Arabian horses, an ice rink, and a pool.

The Lido de Paris' *Revue Bonheur* (2008) was a traditional floorshow that featured musical numbers from previous revues and a cast of 42 Bluebells and 16 Lido boys. The dances included specialty numbers from India (Rasa), and Japan (Noh theatre and Kabuki acrobatics). Haute couture artists François Lesage and Lemarie designed 600 costumes, which required 24 dressing assistants to facilitate the 20 to 30 costume changes per dancer, per show. (Table 1) The modern floorshow in Las Vegas established the physical training and standards for dancers and singers at casino-hotels from the 1950s to the 1990s. Shows produced for today's audiences have smaller casts and are assisted by multimedia scenic devices. The lavish, modern floorshows that were representative of the 1970s American casino showroom are no longer being produced in Las Vegas. The Lido de Paris's press office reports that its final season is scheduled for 2015. The Lido cabaret will be redesigned the following year for a Cirque du Soleil performance.

The Lounge Show Revolution in the U.S.A.

During the 1980s, the Las Vegas floorshow was repackaged into a musical revue with a headliner. Most of these revues revolved around songs written by a particular composer or made famous by a performer such as Ann Margaret, Tina Turner, Juliet Prowse, Mitzi Gaynor, or Cher. Other musical revues focused on specialty acts like magicians Siegfried and Roy, whose program also included an ensemble of dancers.

The floorshow's decline in the 1990s was due to the rising popularity of rock concerts, television variety shows, and touring Broadway shows. The floorshow's influence on other performing arts was obvious in the Hacienda Casino Hotel's *Spice on Ice* (1978), and *Fire on Ice* (1990) shows, which featured ice-dancing teams of showgirls in a musical revue with guest stars such as singer Susan Anton and comedian Redd Foxx. The Wynn Las Vegas's *Le Rêve* (2013) features 87 performers in an aquatic show of aerial-acrobatics in a water-ballet, with a synchronized dive team. The MGM Grand Hotel and Casino in Las Vegas established a sentimental experience by installing a complete replica of the original 1951 Crazy Horse Saloon and Cabaret as the venue for Philippe Decoufle's *Desirs* (2009) from Paris and another show, *Crazy Girls* (2013). *Absinthe* (2013) at Caesar's Palace is a floorshow described by www.Vegas.com as "an adults-only, circus-style spectacle that combines old world burlesque performed by an ensemble of dancers, acrobats, and hosted by an MC."

The modern floorshow performer has gone beyond physically challenging routines with 60 dancers moving in syncopation to more intense physical feats. This style of performance started at Circus Maximus in Valencia, Spain, in 2007, and featured elements of the floorshow as an ensemble of aerial-silk artists (also known as aerial contortionists) to perform hanging from the ceiling by a strip of fabric.

Jubilee! (2013) is a current revival of the traditional floorshow at Bally's Casino and Hotel in Las Vegas. *Jubilee!* is a seven-act, musical revue based on Hollywood historical epics such as *Samson and Delilah* and *Titanic*. The show also features the music of Cole Porter, a large ensemble of 100 performers, topless showgirls, and a thousand costumes designed by Pete Menefee and Bob Mackie. The renaissance of floorshows in the United States—particularly in New Orleans, Seattle, Philadelphia, Orlando, Portland, and Tulsa—is being fueled by a new generation of performers who reinterpret the old forms in various music and theatre venues.

Table 1

History of Shows at the Lido de Paris Theatre, Paris, France

1946 Sans rimes, ni raisons	1961 Pour vous
1946 Mississippi	1962 Suivez moi
1947 Made in Paris	1964 Quelle nuit
1948 Confetti	1966 Pourquoi pas ?
1949 Bravo	1969 Grand Prix
1950 Enchantment	1971 Bonjour la nuit
1951 Rendezvous	1973 Grand Jeu
1953 Voilà	1977 Allez Lido
1954 Désirs	1981 Cocorico
1955 Voulez-vous	1985 Panache
1956 C'est Magnifique	1990 Bravissimo
1957 Prestige	1994 C'est Magique
1959 Avec Plaisir	2003 Bonheur

Source: Lido de Paris, Paris France, Lido Press; web; 2012.

The University of Nevada at Las Vegas offers an annual public exhibition of its Donn Arden collection of theatrical memorabilia, costumes, and museum-quality art which was dedicated to the city of Las Vegas for scholars and performers of the floorshow as a theatrical art. The author of this thesis developed a website called *Floorshow* in 2012 to present archival footage, photography, and ongoing coverage of floorshows. It can be viewed at *https://sites.google.com/a/zips.uakron.edu/the-floorshow*. The site features links to cabaret websites in Paris, an archive with photographs of ensemble casts, promotional video footage and soundtracks in French without English translation or subtitles, and access to the beginning of an online lecture series. The website displays vintage posters, programs, and photos featuring various dignitaries and celebrities who attended the shows.

BIBLIOGRAPHY

"// LIDO // Champs Elysees Avenue Paris : Music Hall Cabaret, Spectacle, Dancing Show, Restaurant." *// LIDO // Champs Elysees Avenue Paris : Music Hall Cabaret, Spectacle, Dancing Show, Restaurant*. N.p., n.d. Web. 12 June 2012. <http://www.lido.fr/us/>.

Bogart, Anne. *A Director Prepares: Seven Essays on Art and Theatre*. London: Routledge, 2001. Print.

Brockett, Oscar Gross, and Franklin J. Hildy. *History of the Theatre*. Boston: Pearson, 2008. Print.

Bryant, Betty. *Here Comes the Showboat!* Lexington, KY: University of Kentucky, 1994. Print.

Cars, Guy Des. *Le Fabuleux roman du Lido de Paris*. 1986. Lido Press. Print.

Cass, Joan. *The Dance: A Handbook for the Appreciation of the Choreographic Experience*. North Carolina: McFarland &, 1999. Print.

DeMille, Agnes, and N. M. Bodecker. *The Book of the Dance*. London: Hamlyn, 1963. Print.

Duke of Saint-Simon. *Memoirs of Louis XIV and the Regency*. Vol. II. Washington & London: M. Walter Dunn, 1901. Print.

Gottlieb, Robert S. *Reading Dance: A Gathering of Memoirs, Reportage, Criticism, Profiles, Interviews, and Some Uncategorizable Extras*. New York: Pantheon, 2008. Print.

Graham, Philip. *Showboat*. Austin & London: University of Texas, 1969. Print.

Guest, Ivor. *The Ballet of the Enlightenment: The Establishment of the Ballet D'action in France, 1770-1793*. London: Dance, 1996. Print.

Hanners, John. *"It Was Play or Starve": Acting in the Nineteenth Century American Popular Theatre*. Bowling Green: Bowling Green State University Popular, 1993. Print.

Macy, Robert, and Melinda Macy. *The Stars of Las Vegas: The Entertainment Capital of the World : Through the Years*. Las Vegas, NV: M*M Graphics, 2000. Print.

Perry, George C. *Bluebell: The Authorized Biography of Margaret Kelly, Founder Of the Legendary Bluebell Girls*. London: Pavilion, 1986. Print.

ABOUT THE AUTHOR

Douglas William Woods holds a Master of Arts Degree in Theatre Arts from The University of Akron.
The Floorshow: origins of a theatrical art.
Let's dance.

www.ingramcontent.com/pod-product-compliance
Lightning Source LLC
Chambersburg PA
CBHW041832300426
44111CB00002B/60